Turtles Adult Coloring Book

This book belongs to:

____

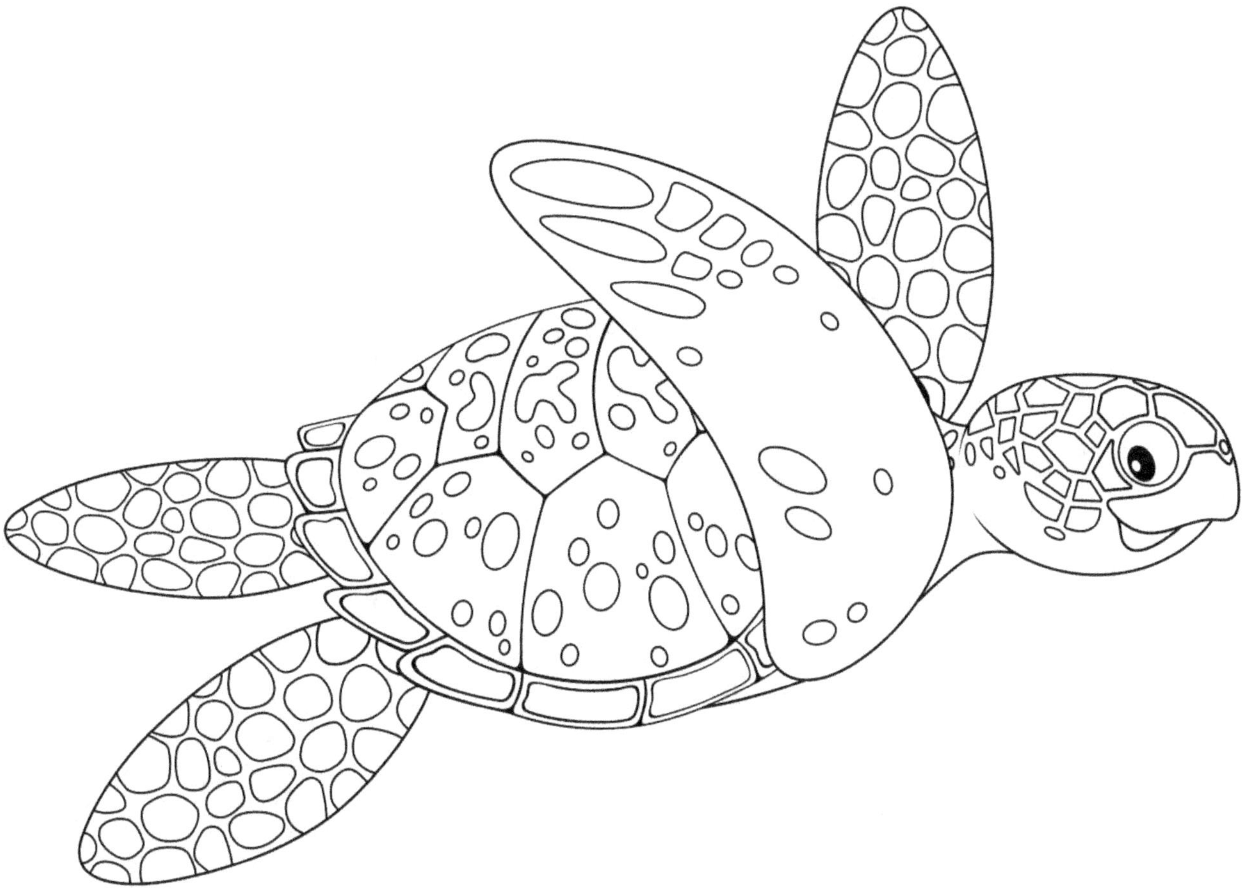

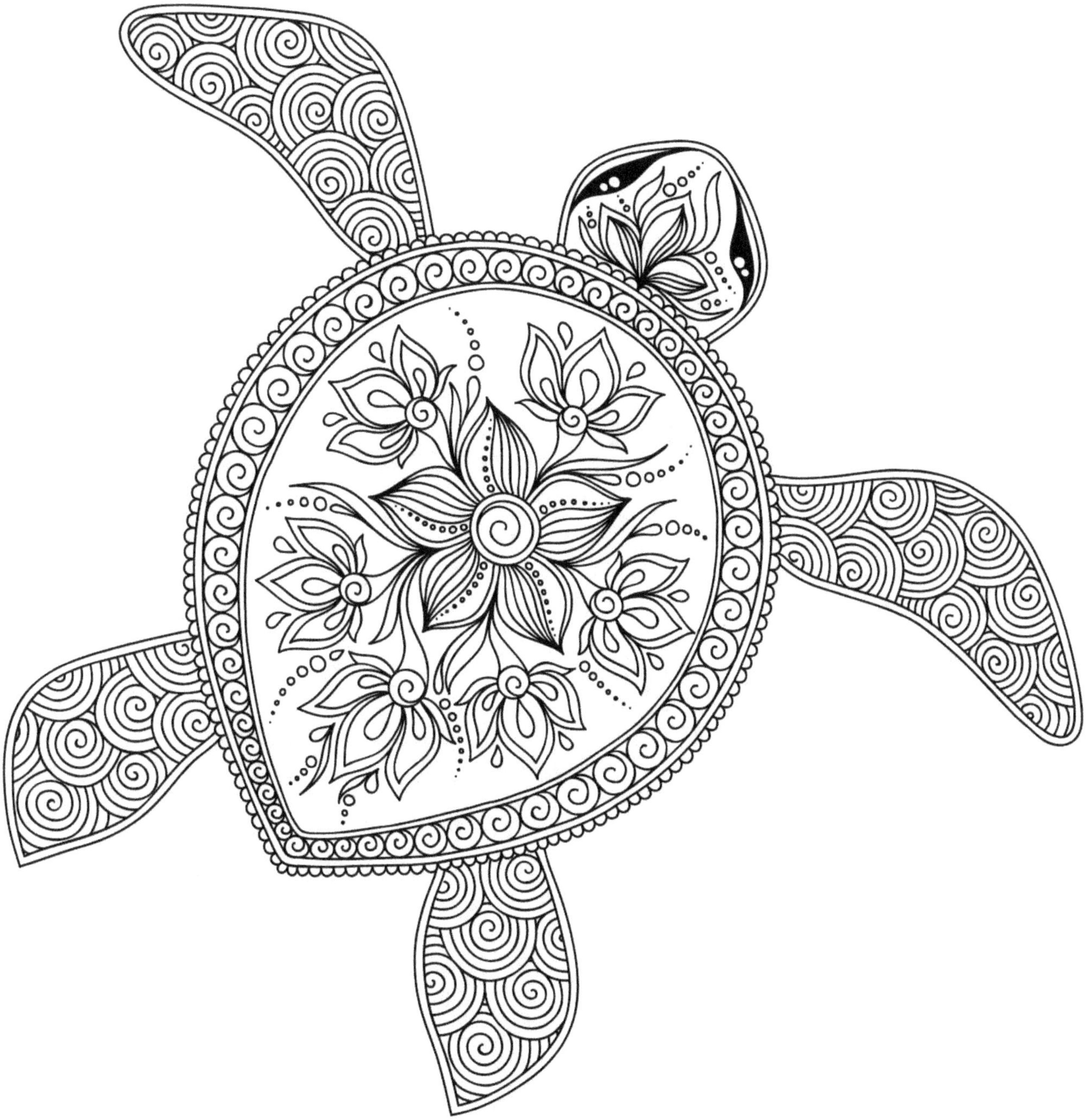

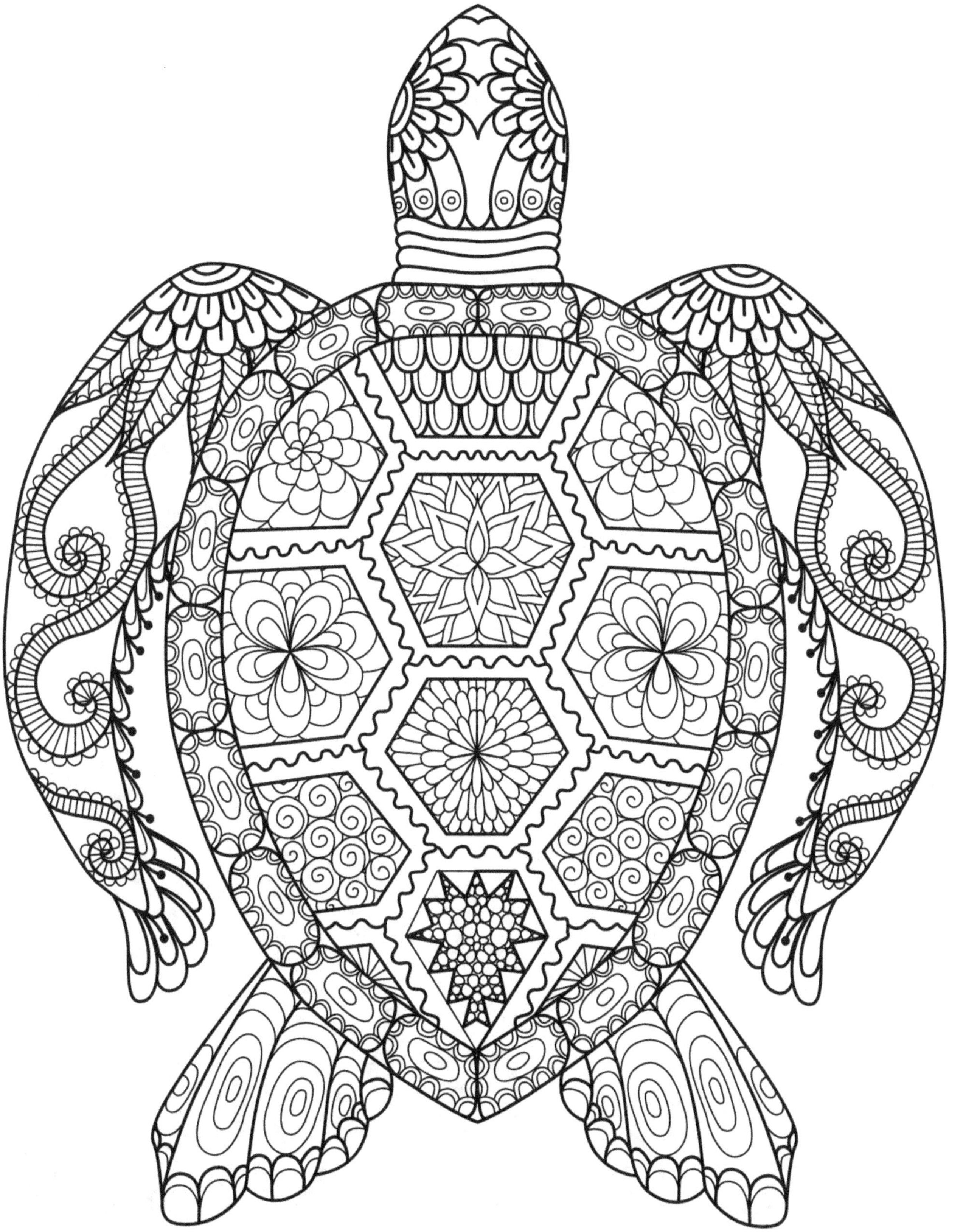

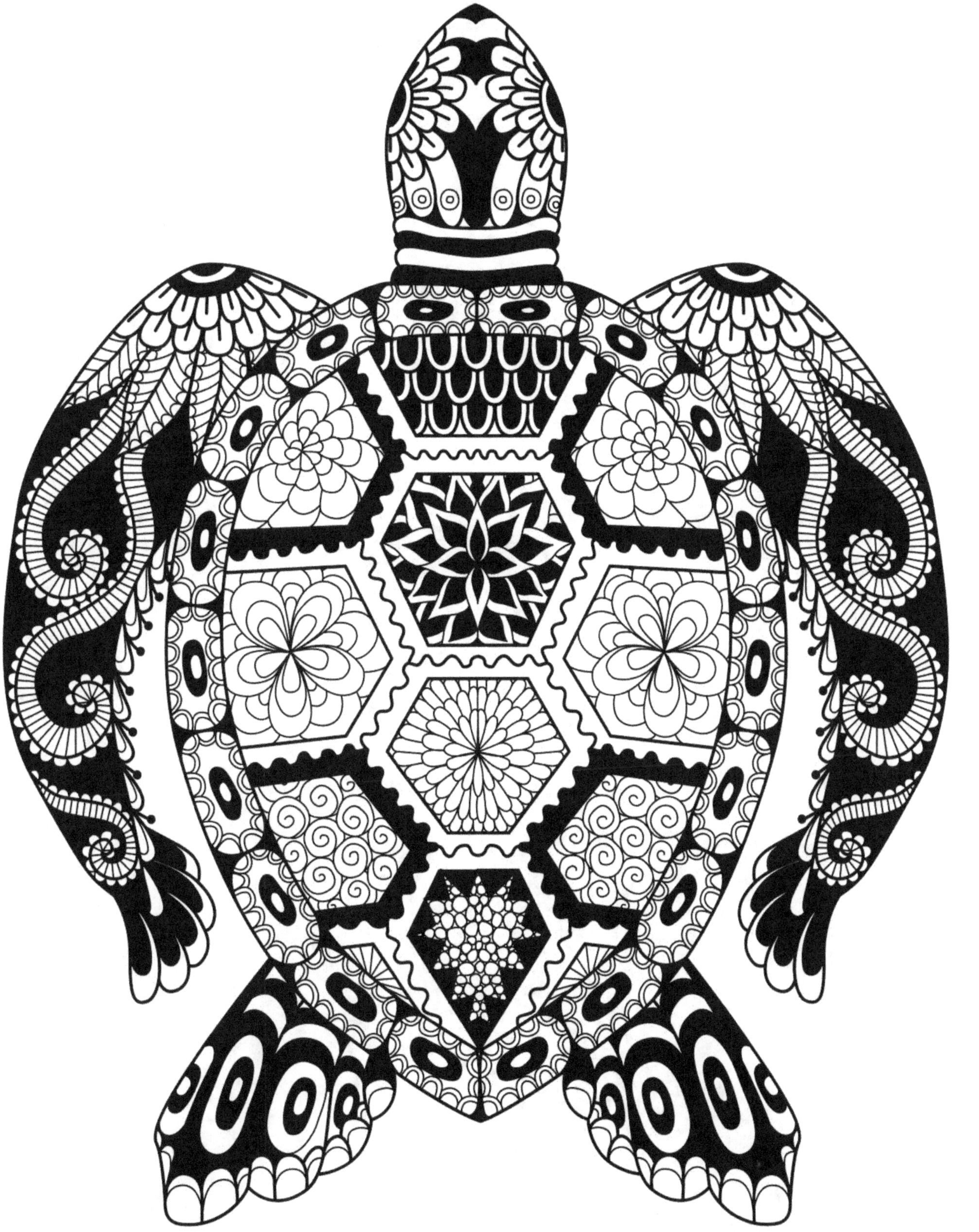

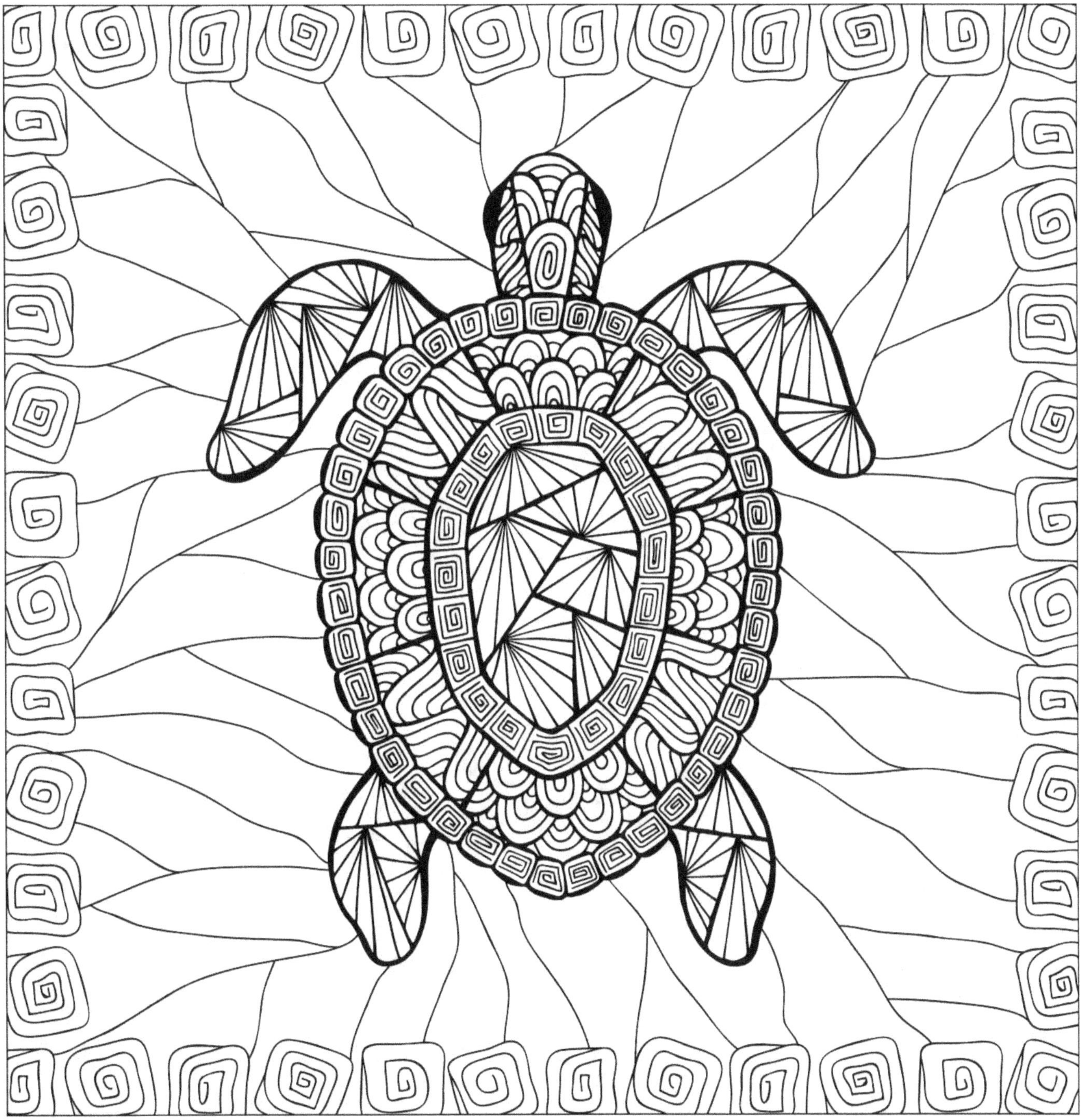

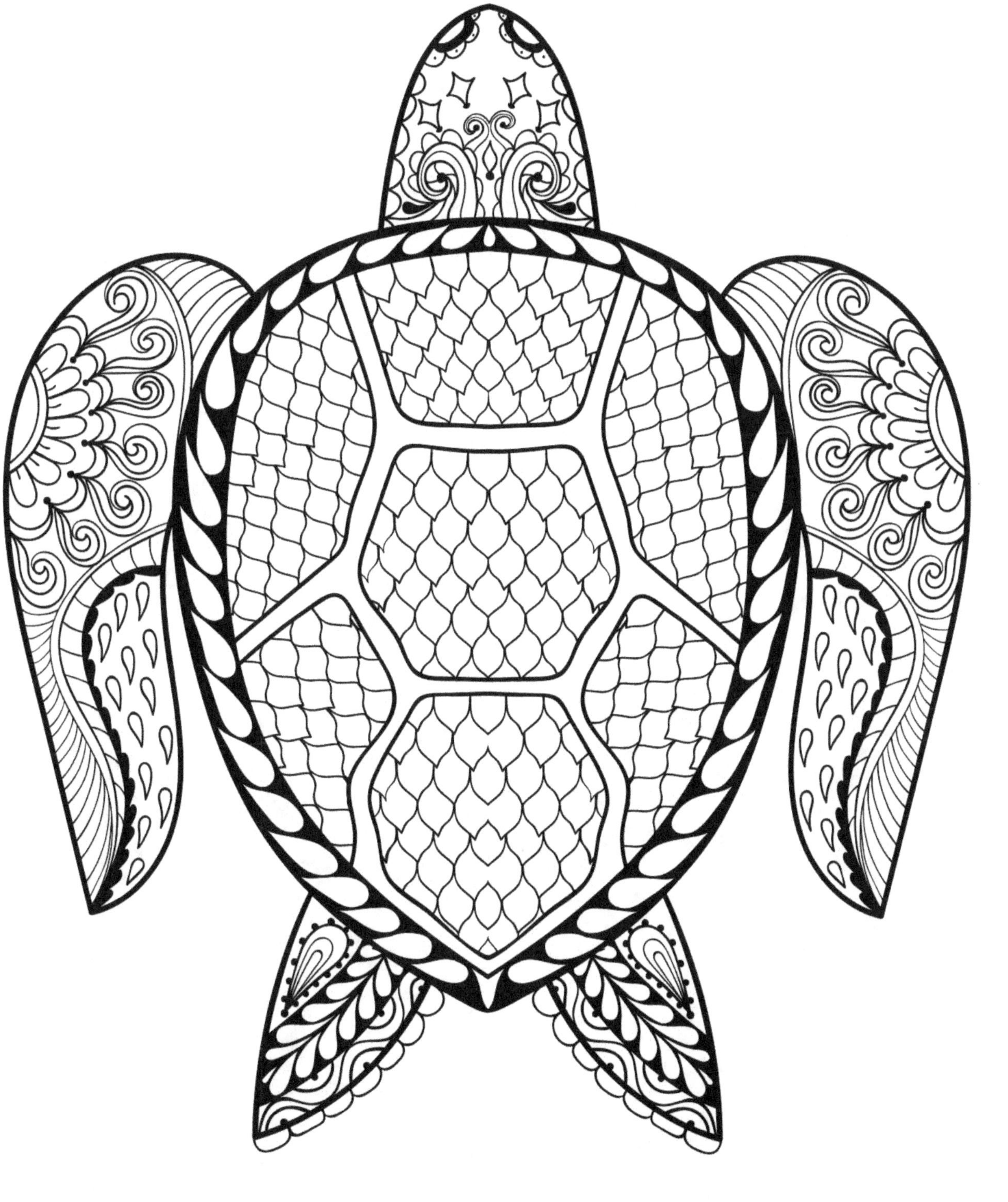

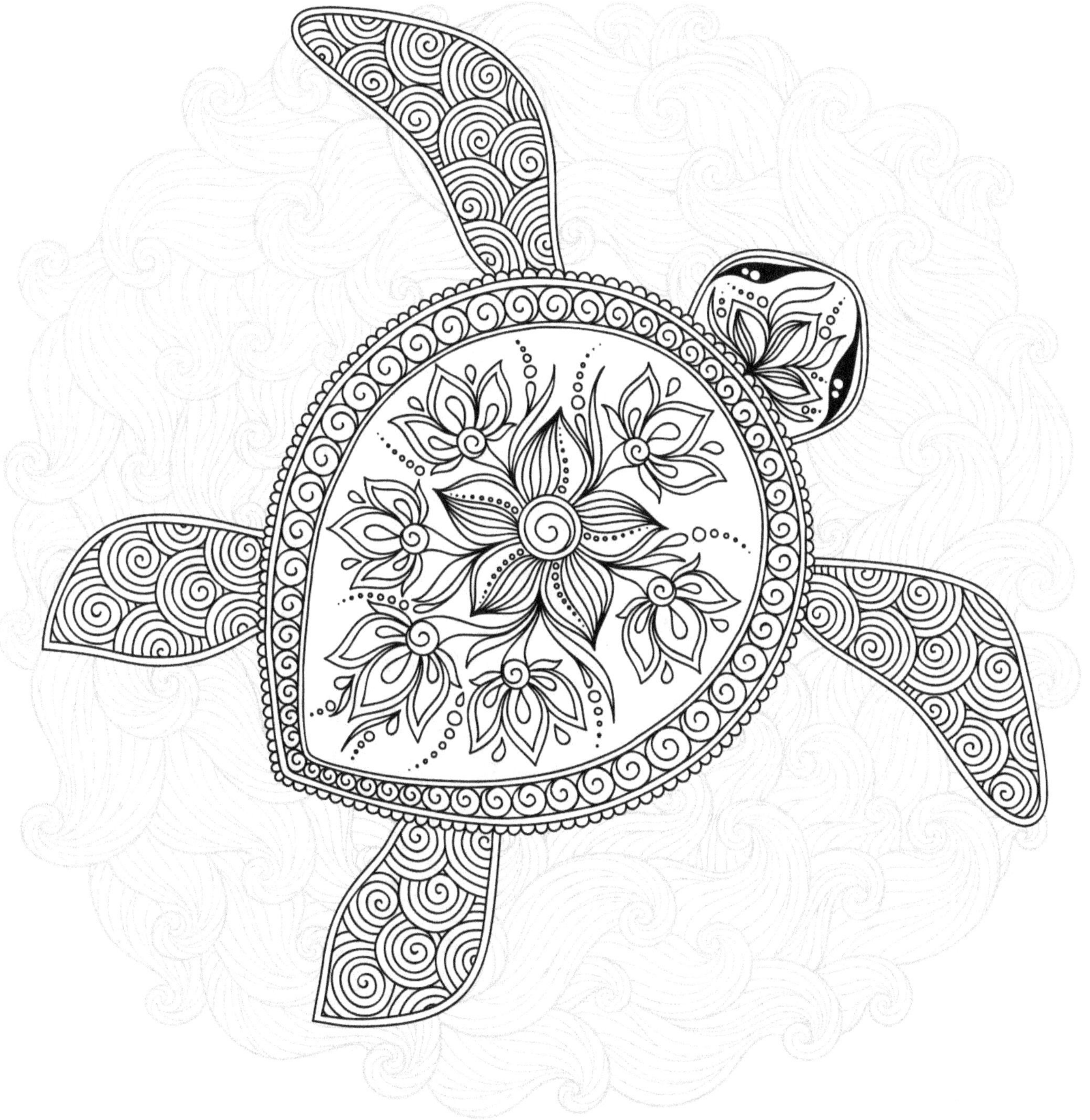

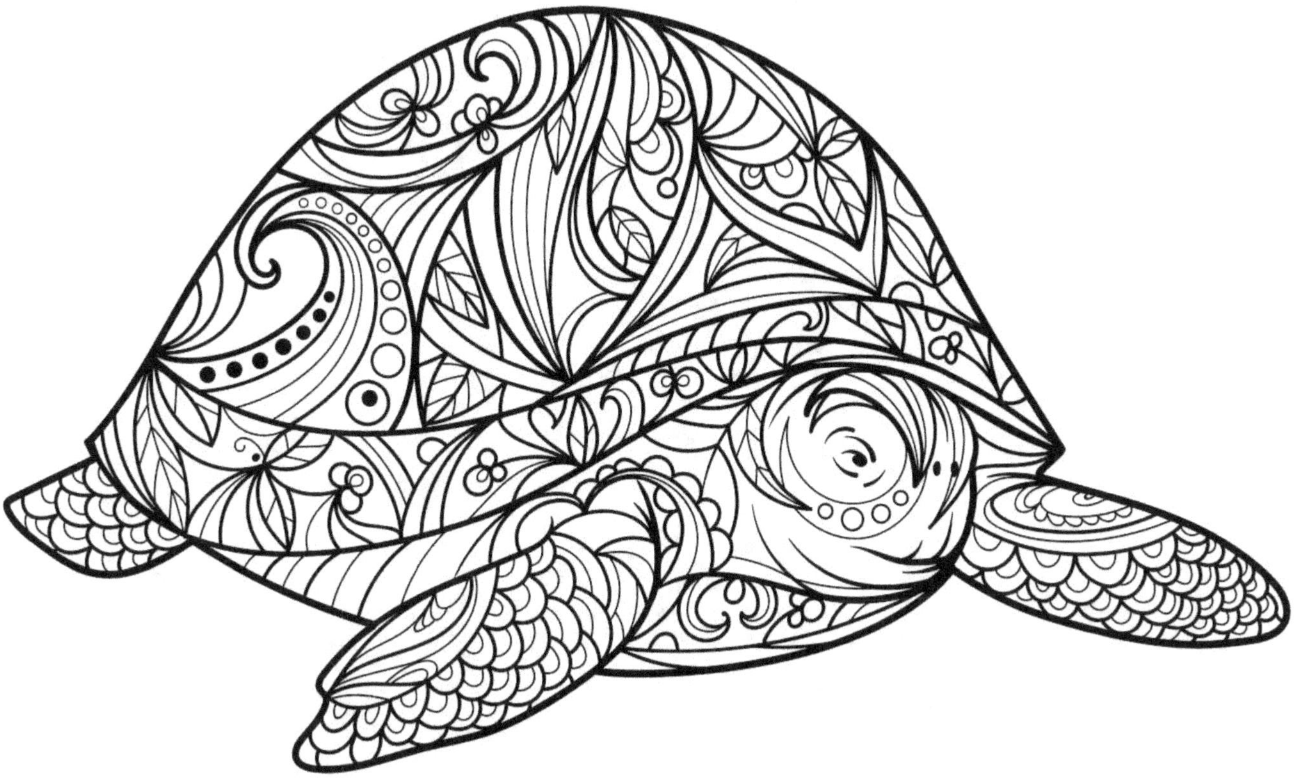

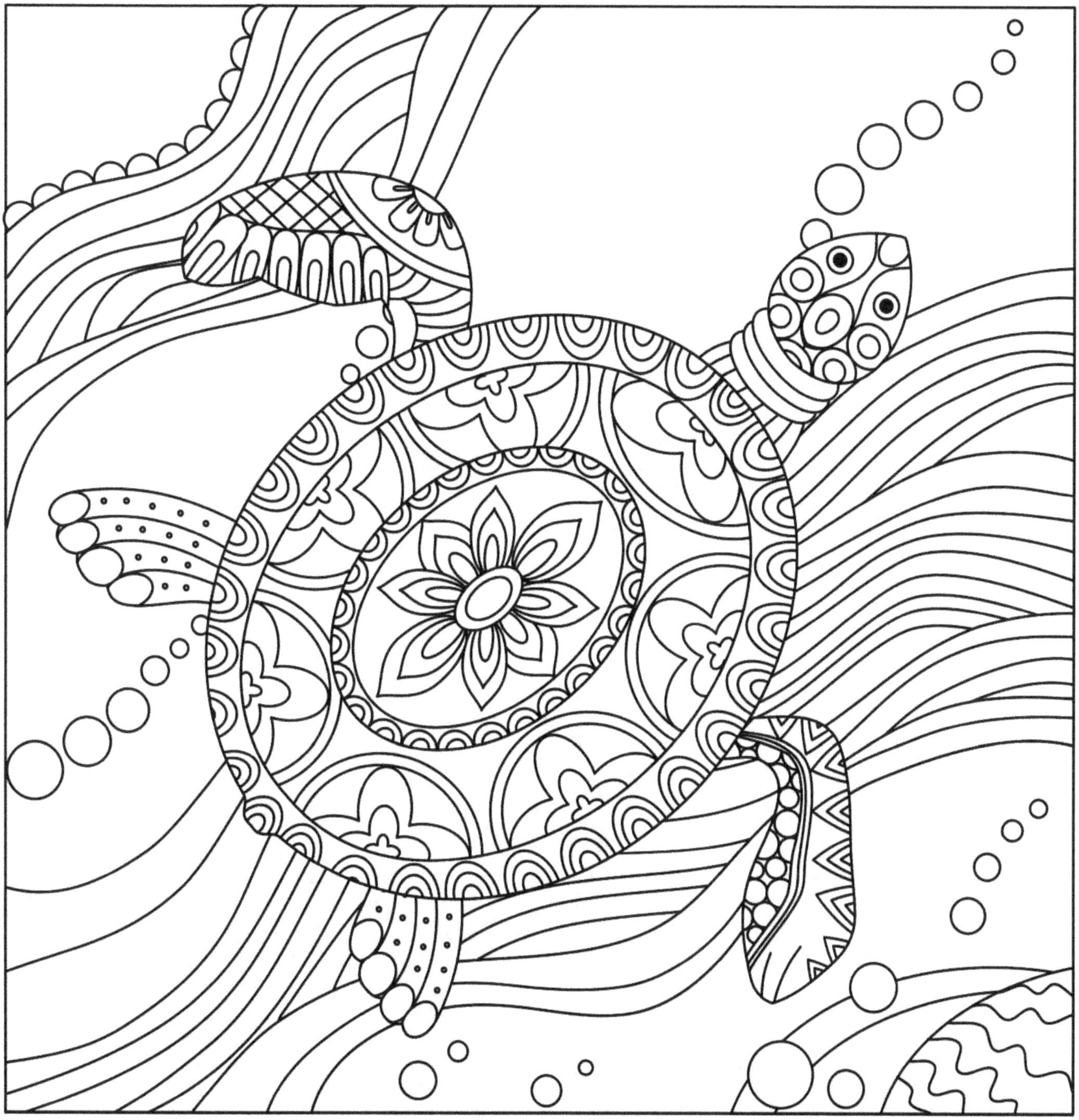

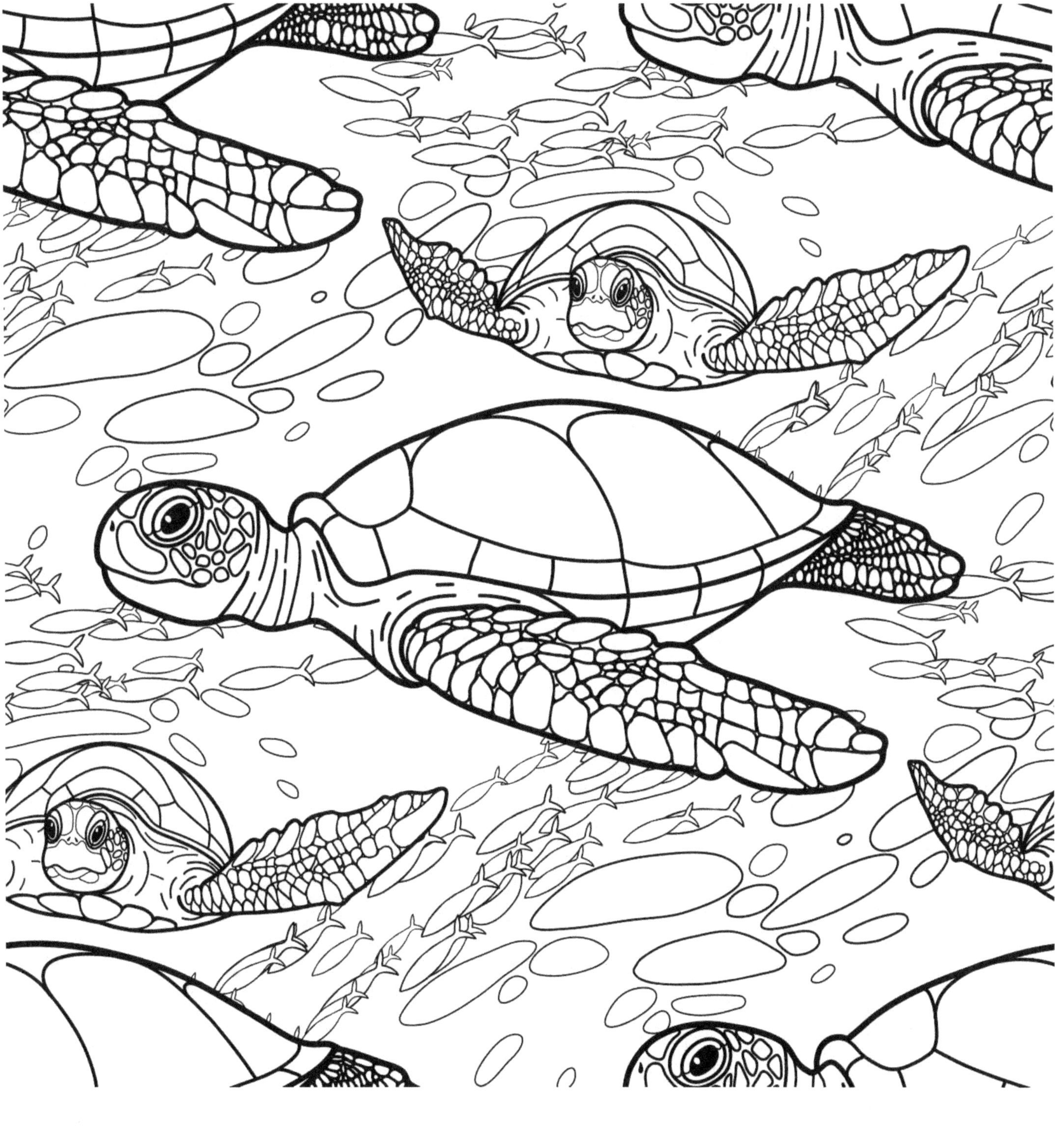

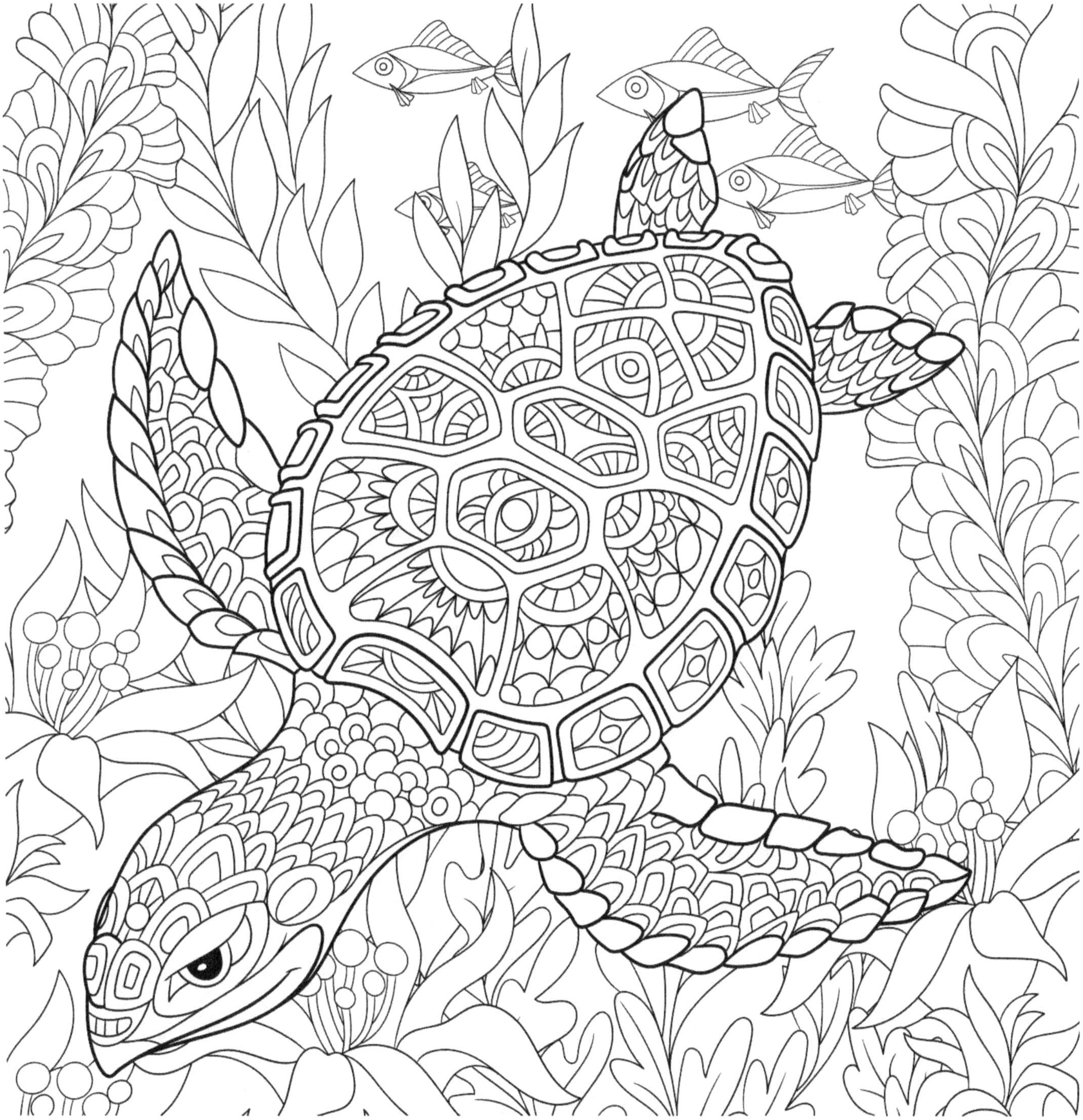

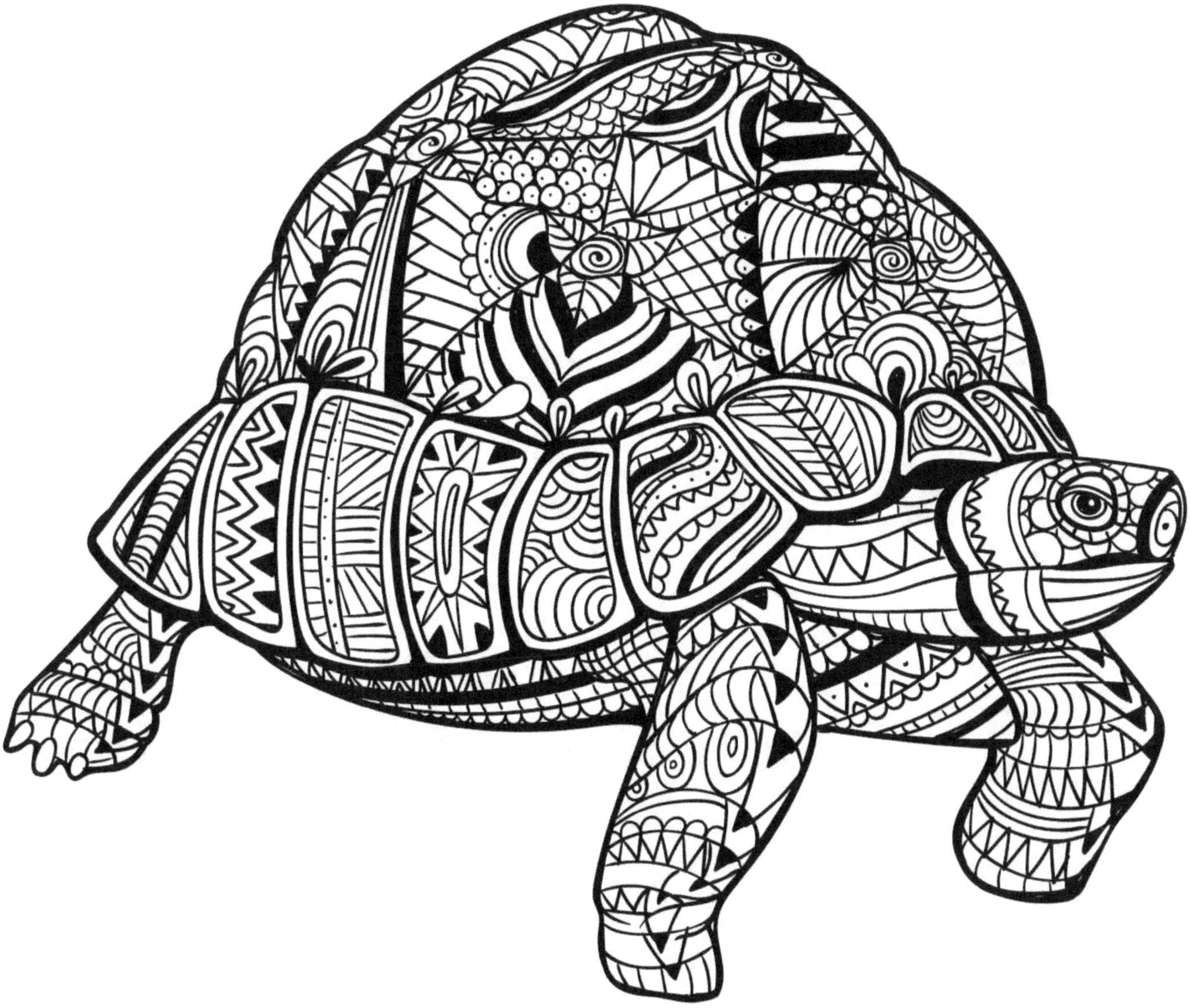

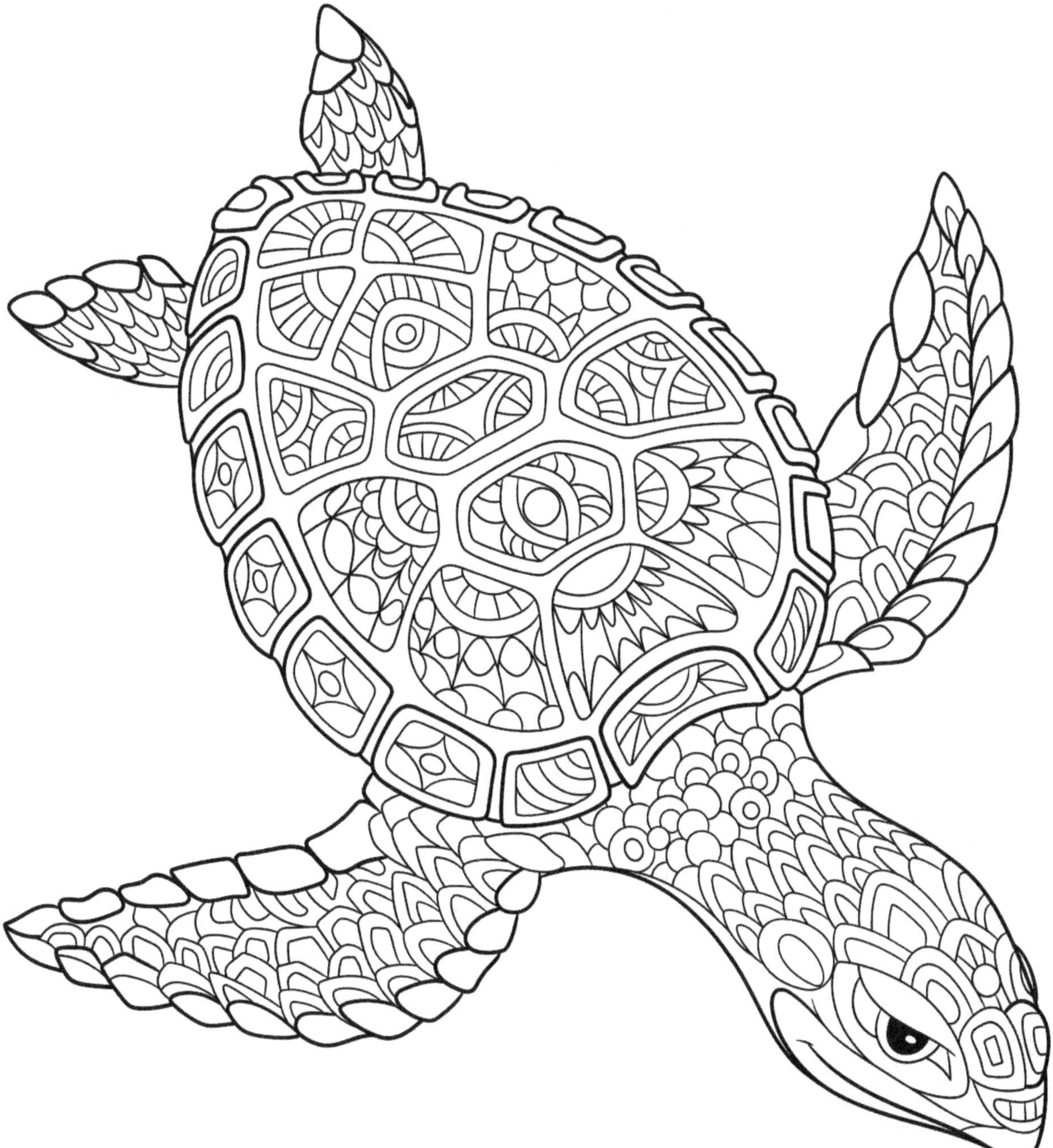

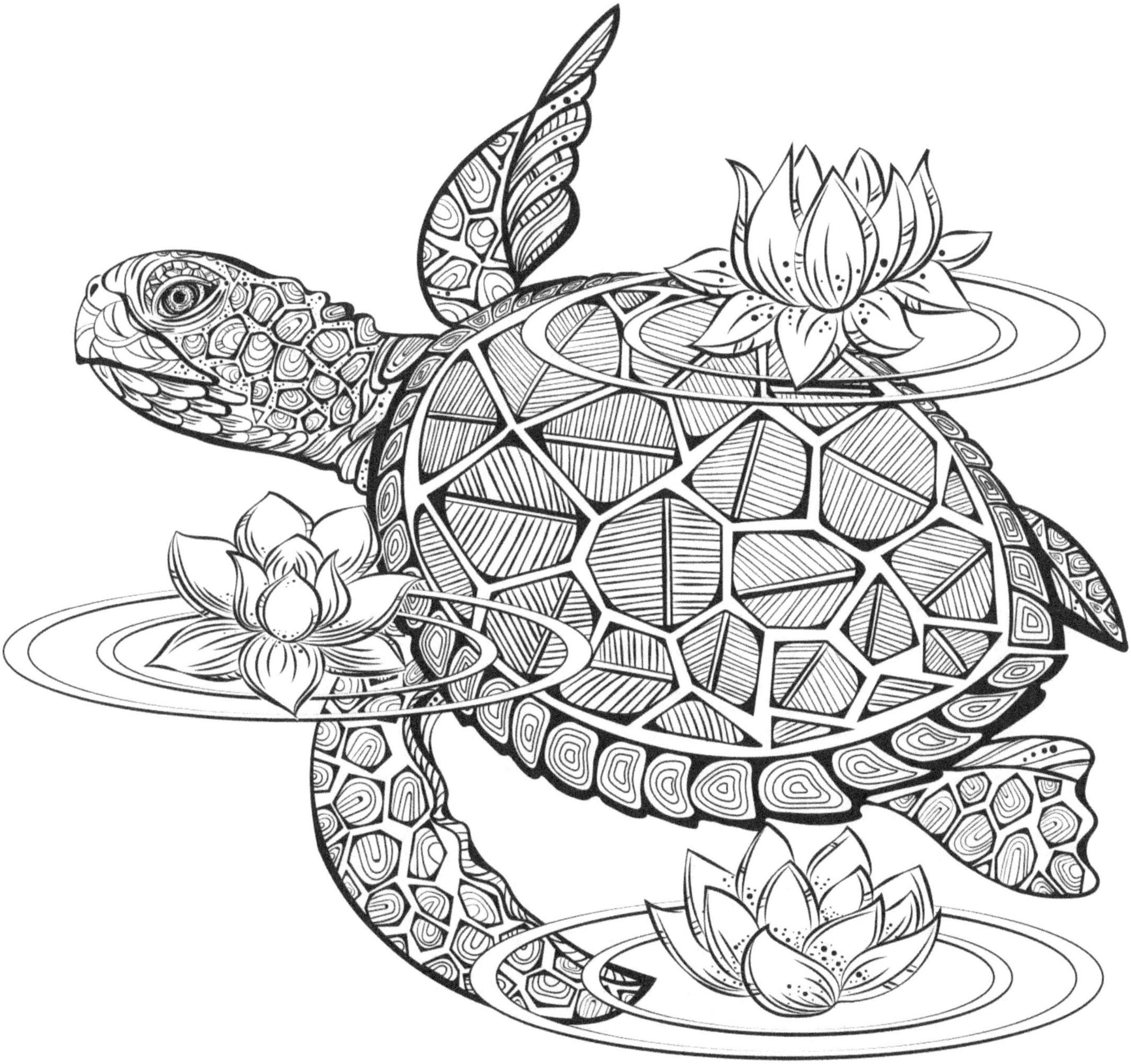

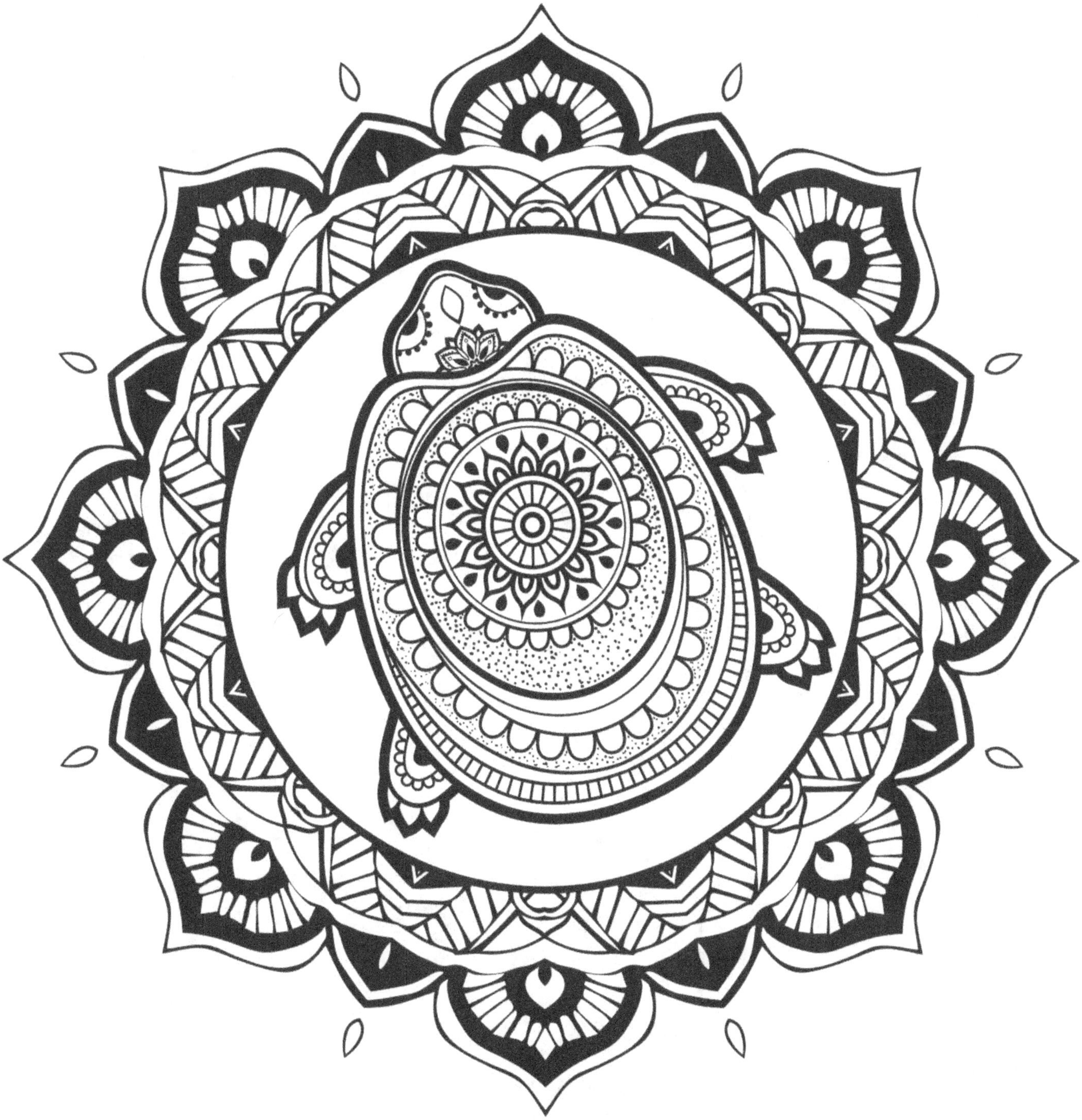

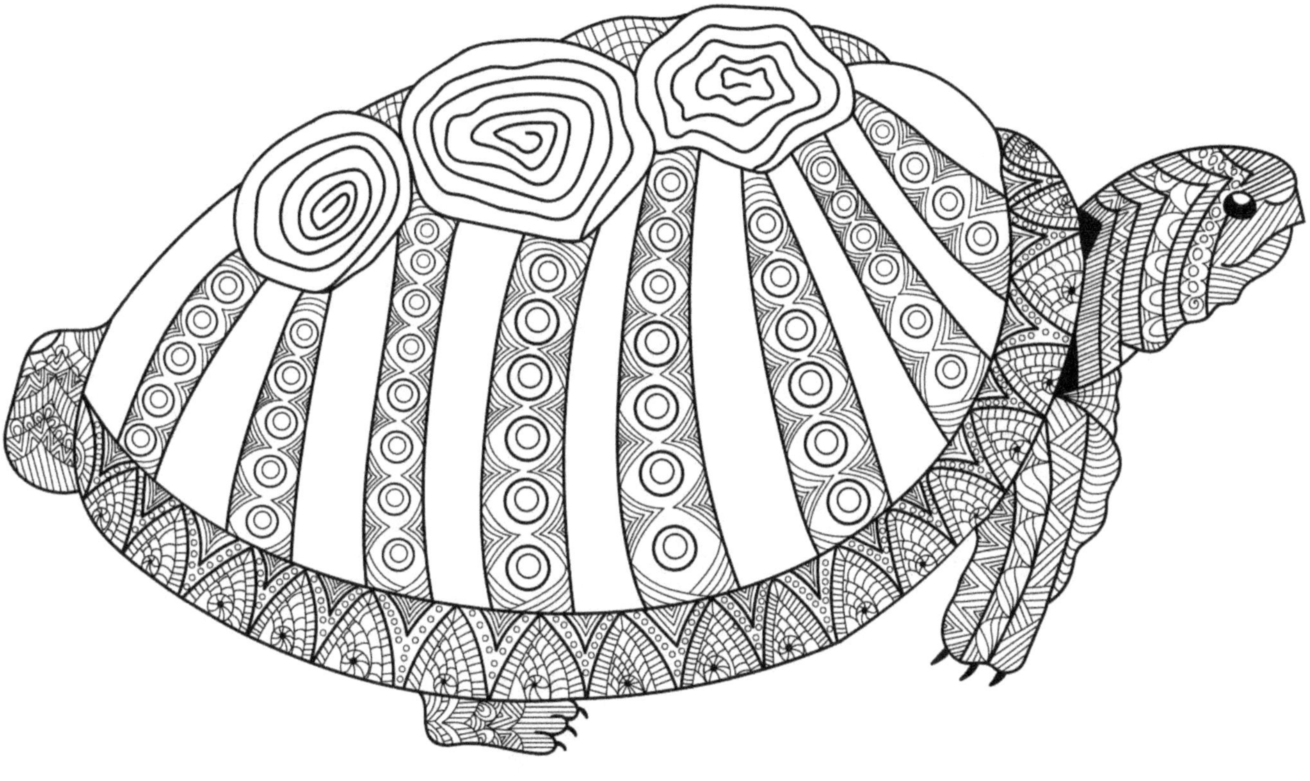

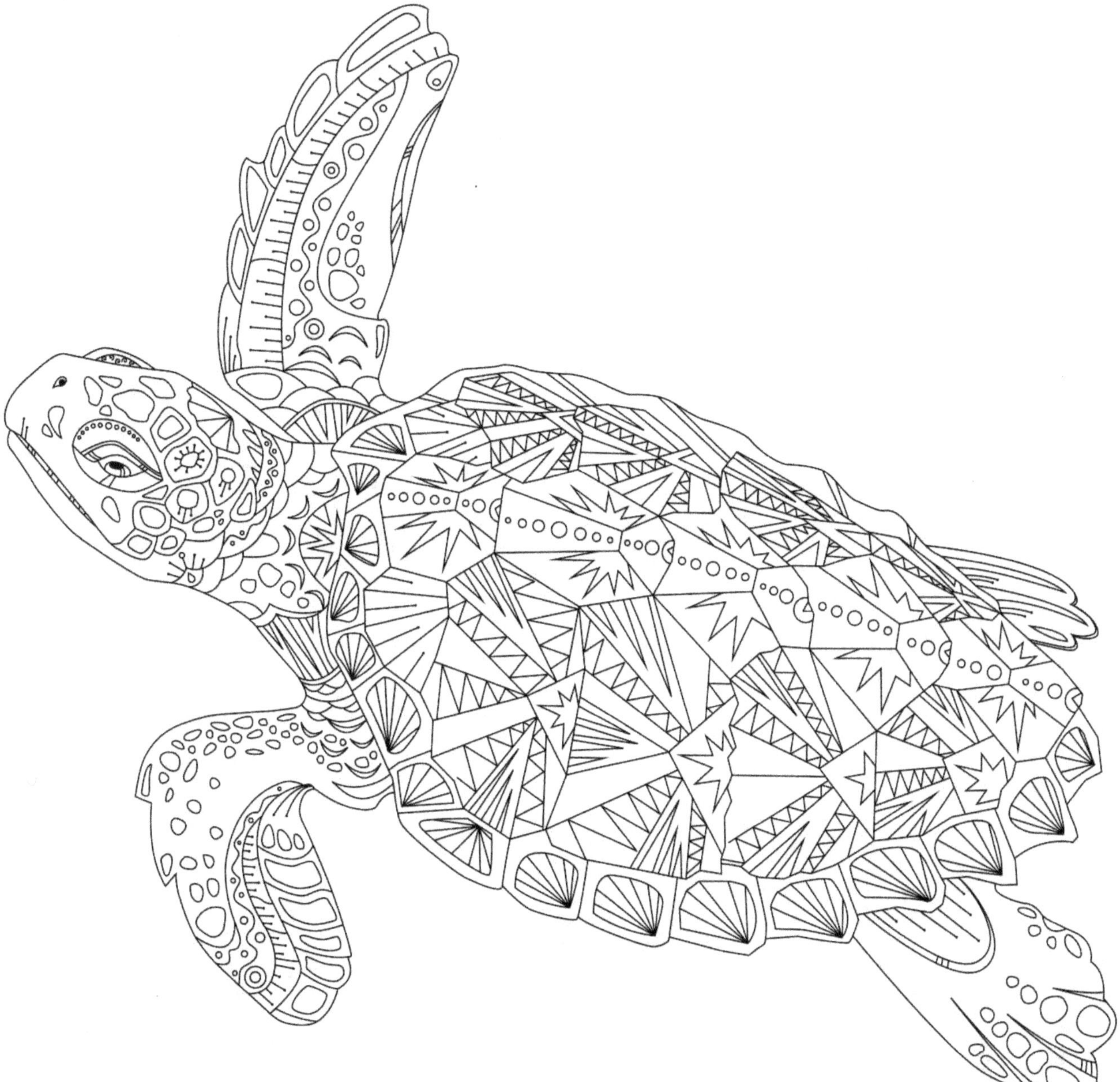

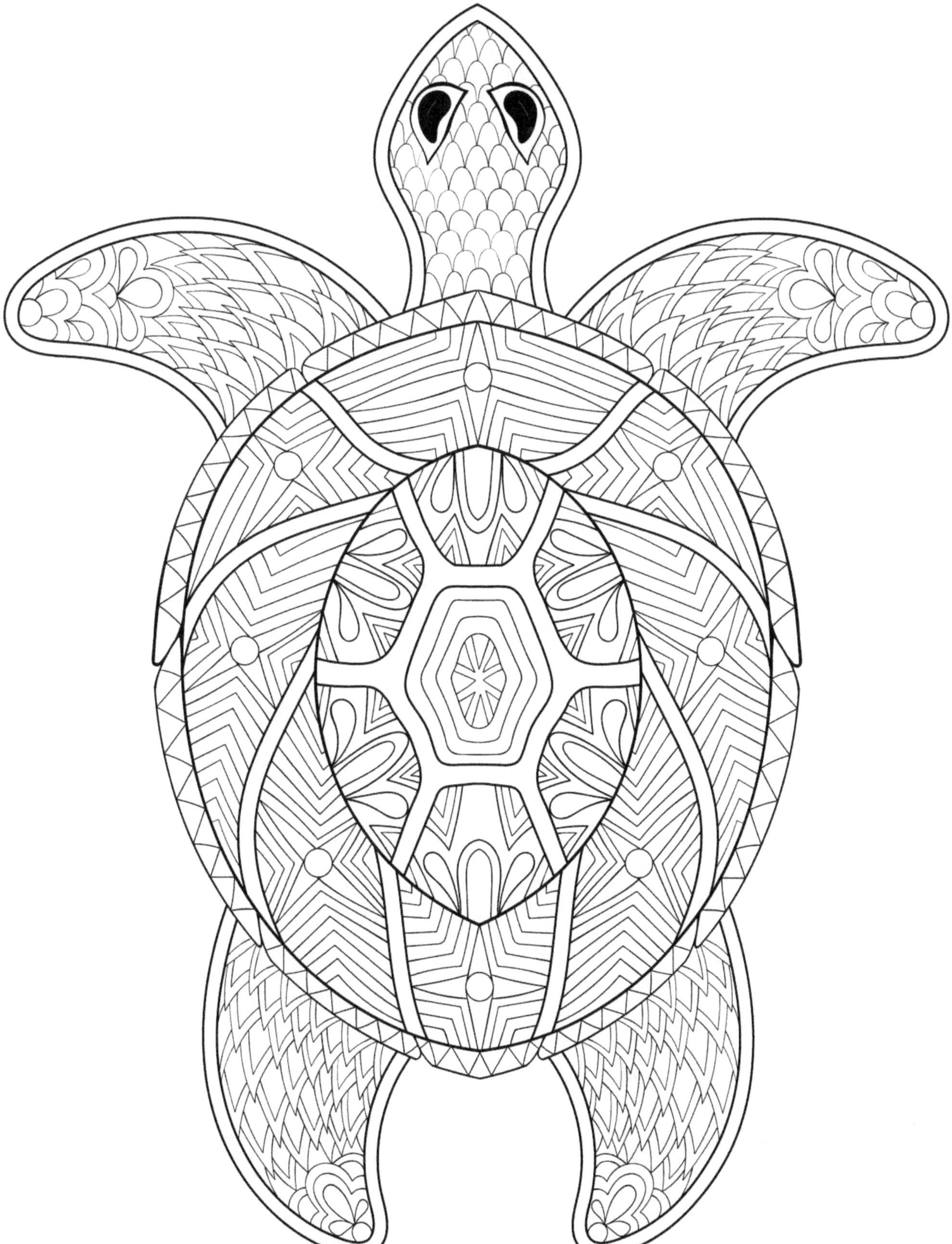

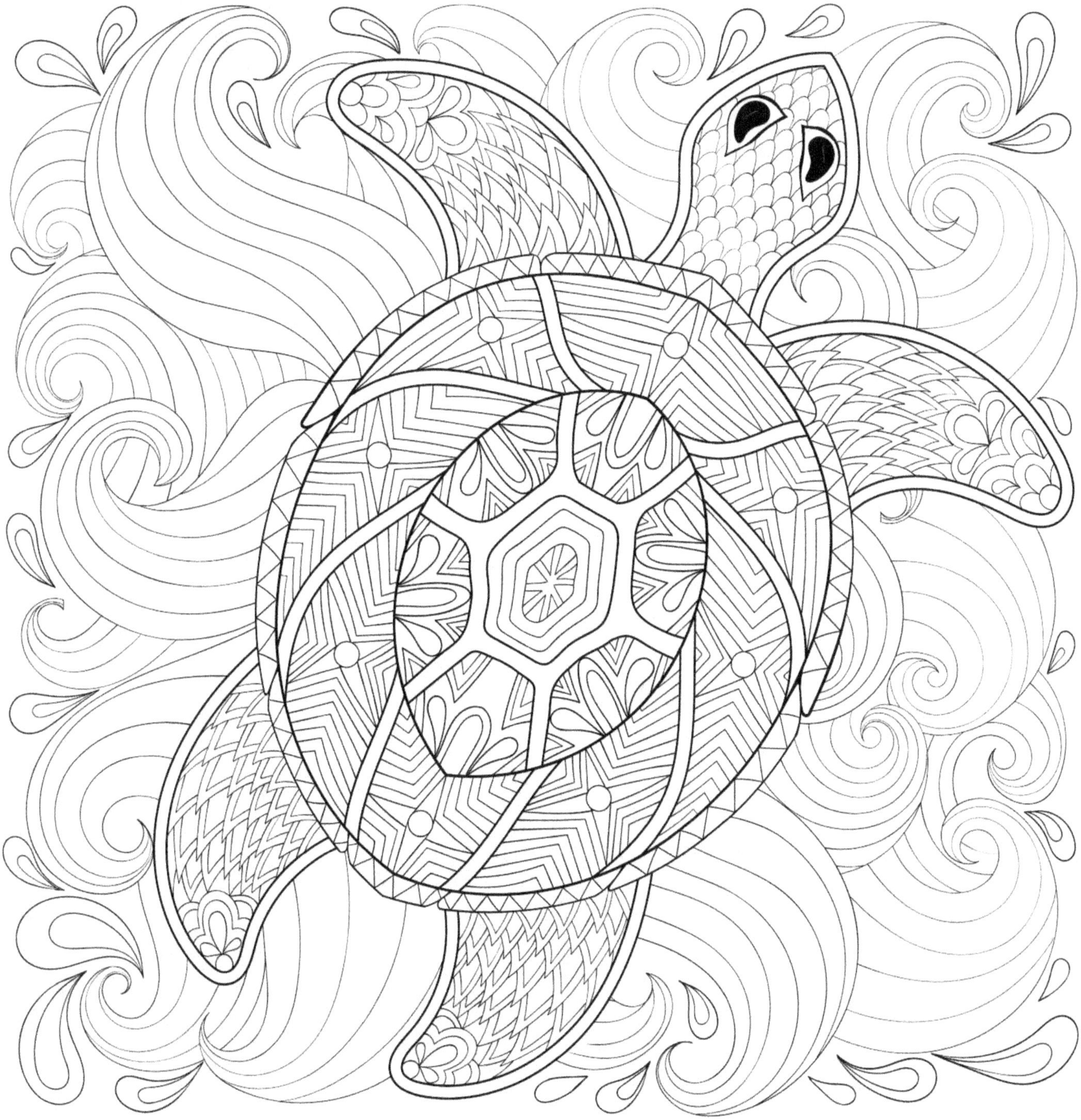

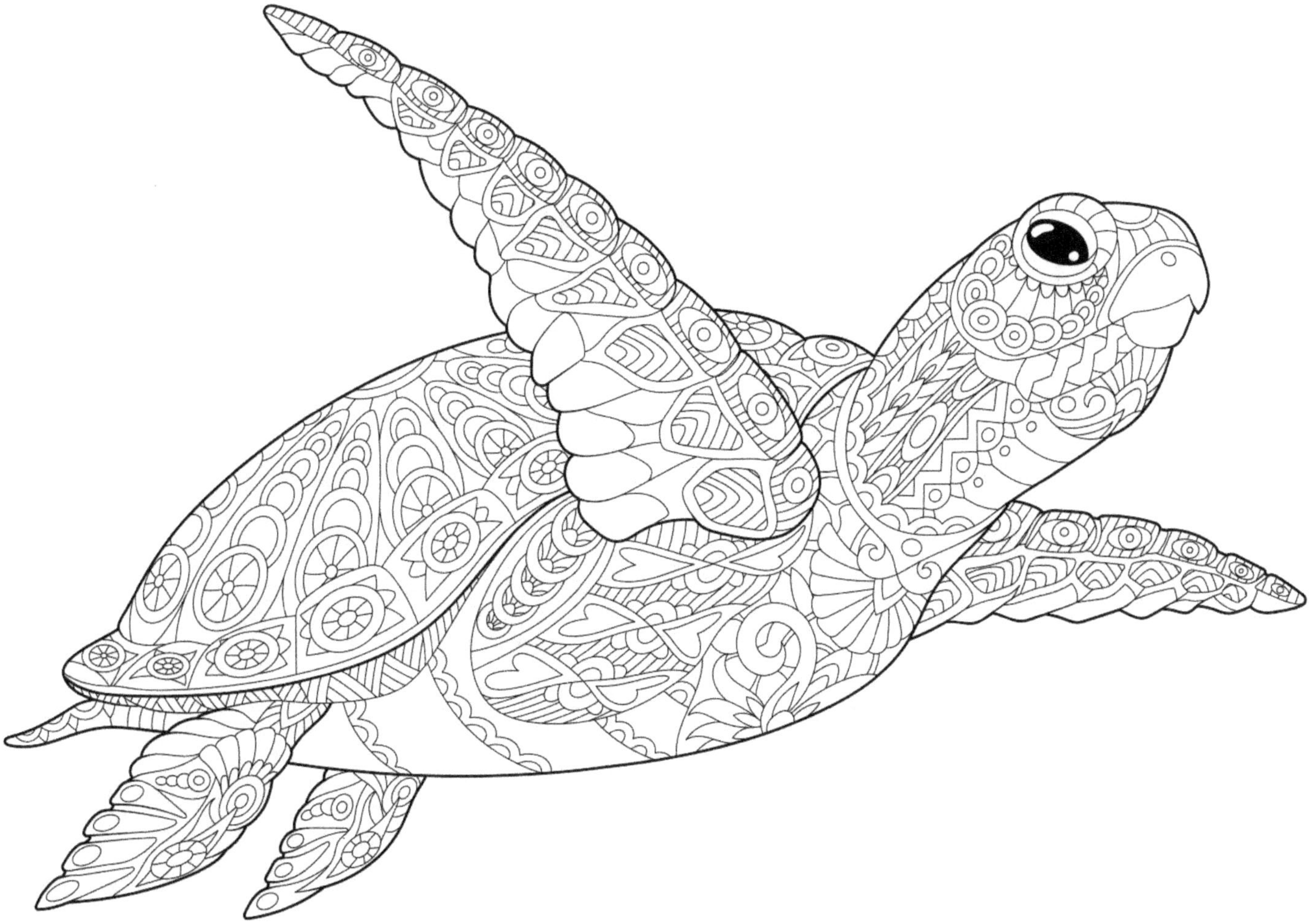

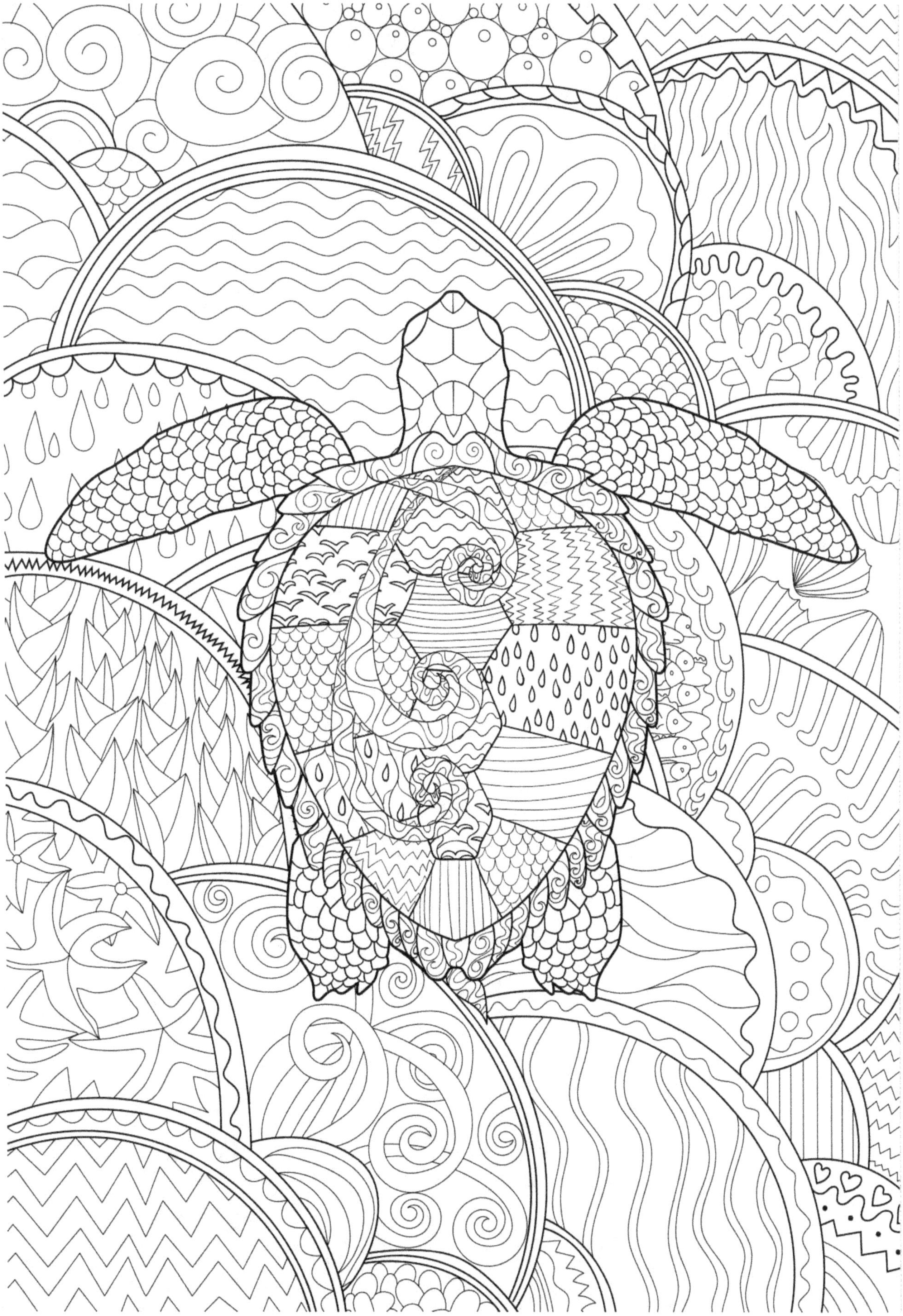

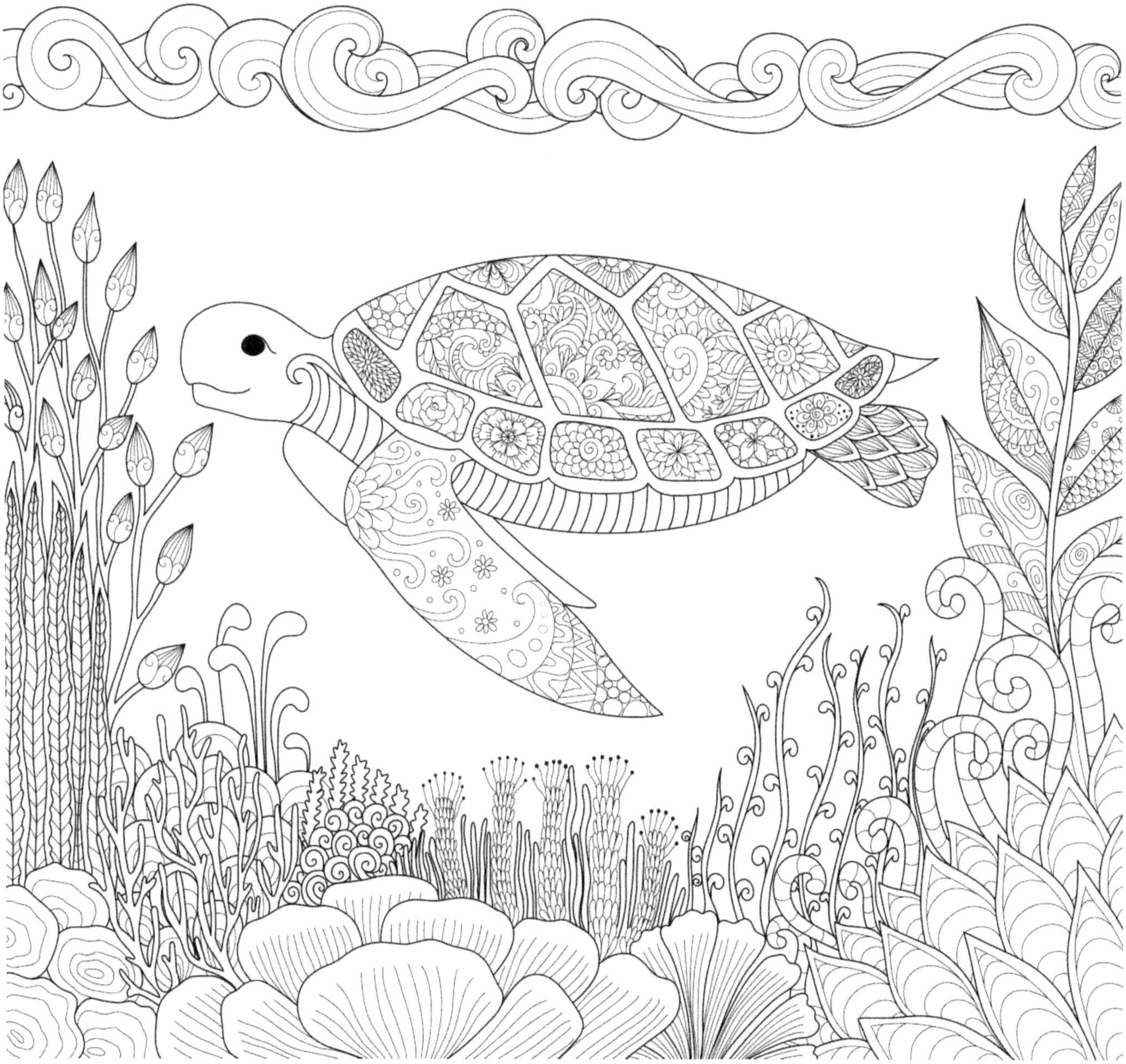

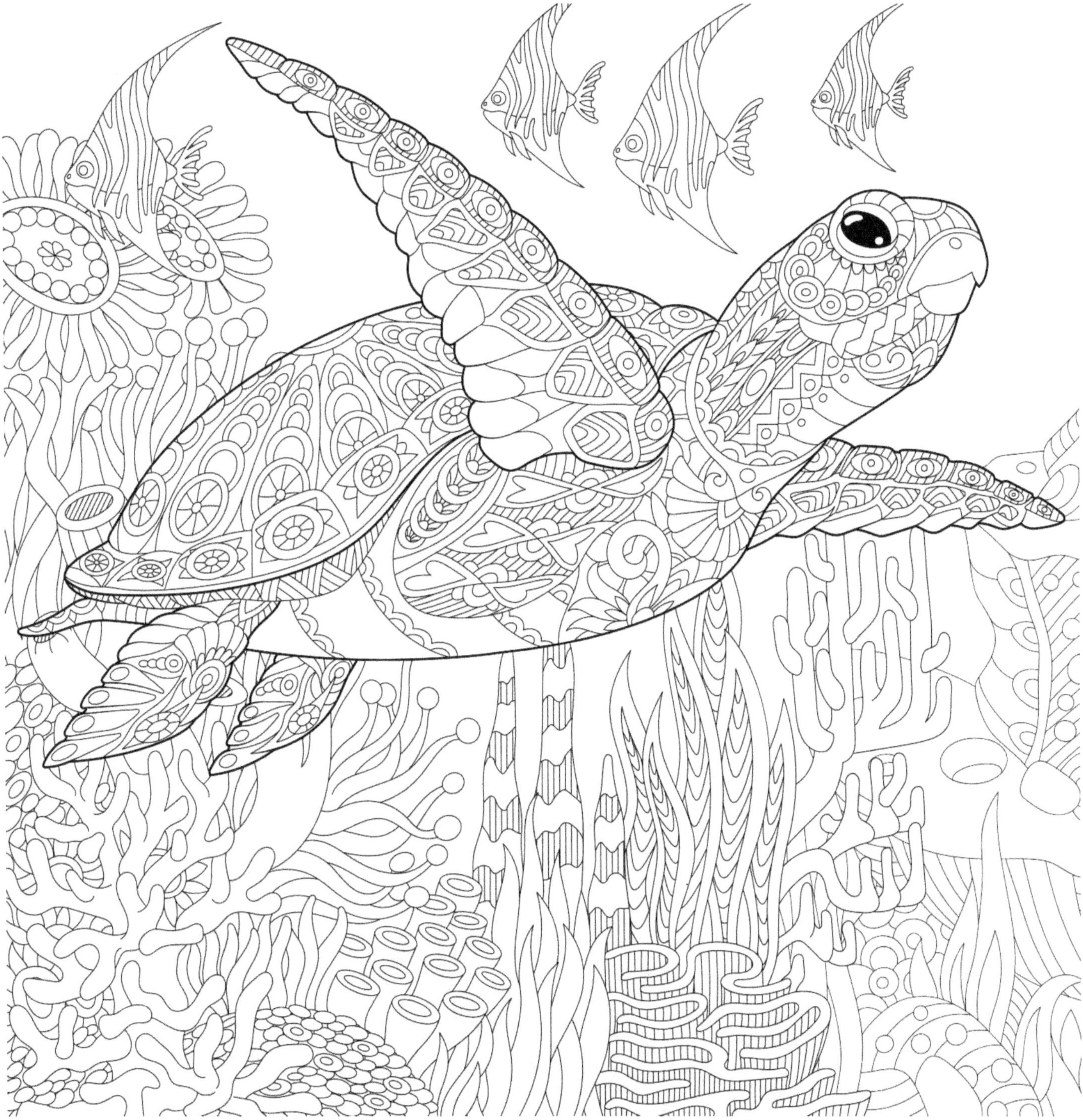

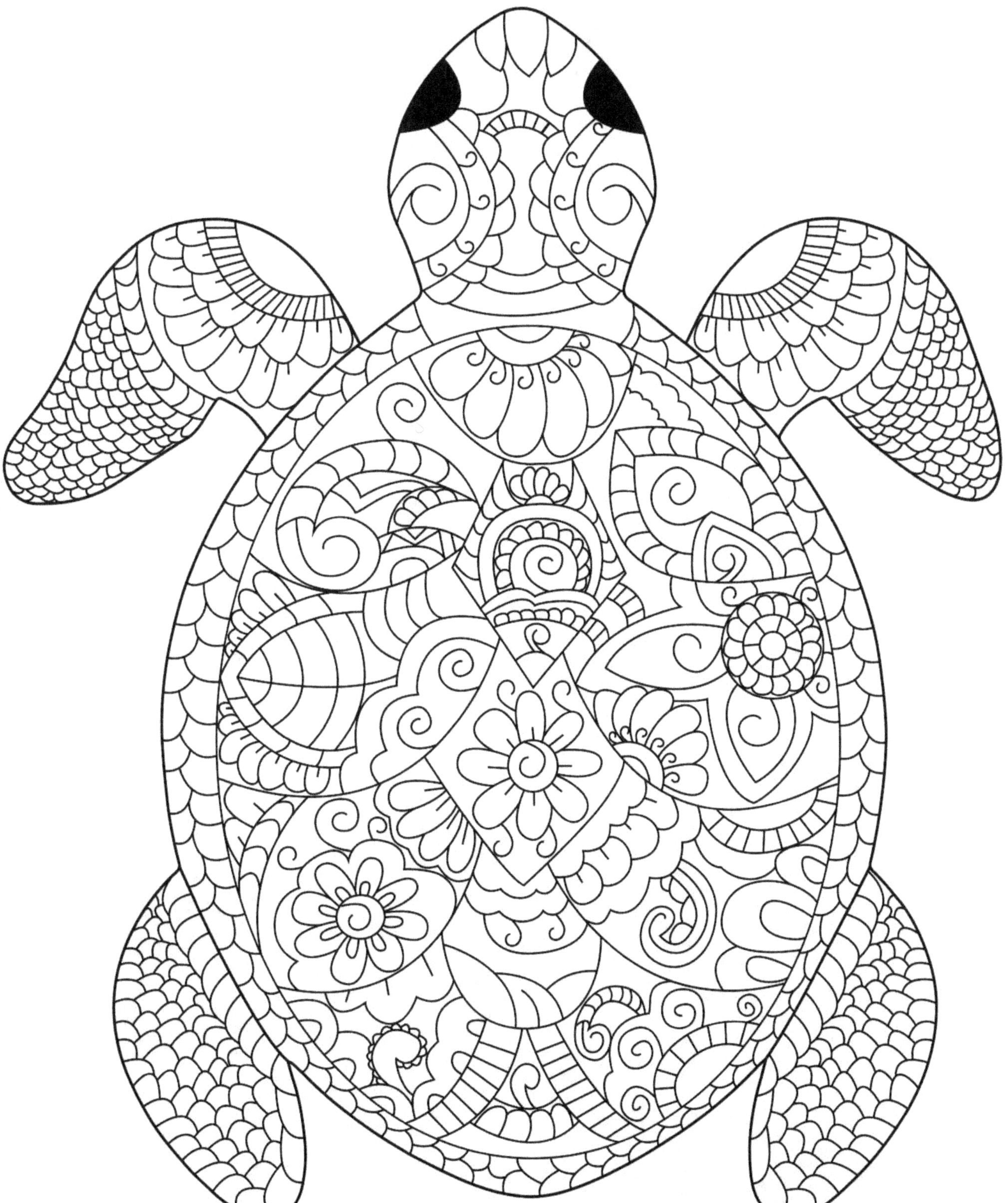

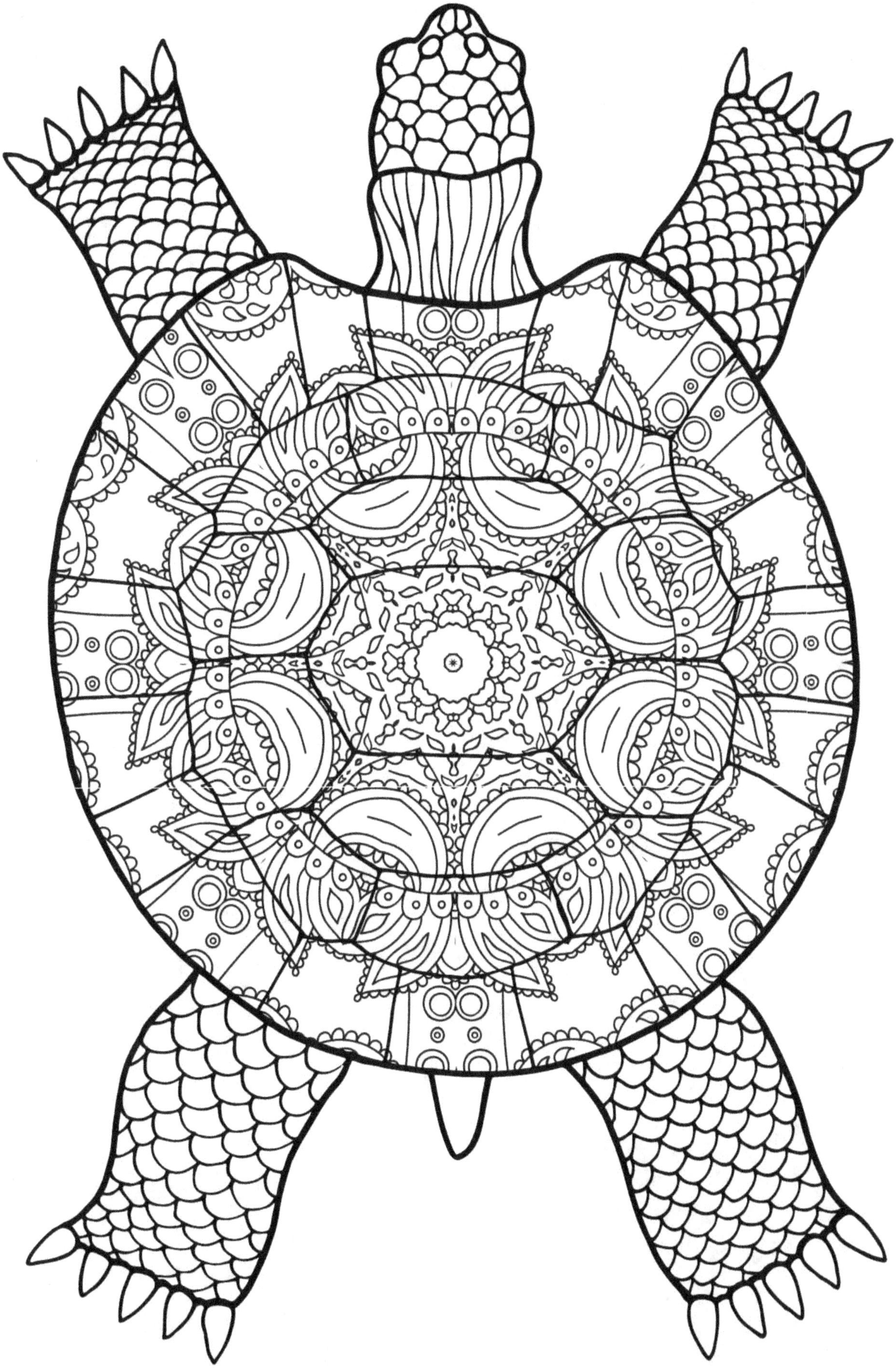